If You Give A Dog A Doobie

Again for Ariel and Sam
-S.M.

Again for Aurora
-M.O.

T0089260

Special Thanks To:

Tosca Miserendino
Stacie Odum
Jack W. Perry
Don Loudon
Ron Riffle
Beverly Miserendino
Travis Bundy
Shawn Gates
Joao Pimentel

If You Give A Dog A Doobie

Written By Sam Miserendino
Illustrated By Mike Odum

Skyhorse Publishing, Inc.

KRUNCHY KREME

If you give a dog a doobie, he'll ask you if there's chocolate in it.

When you tell him
that there's not,

he'll puff…

Puff…

And...uh,
you'll pass.

When he sees
your frisbee,

he'll ask you to throw
it to him.

He'll feel like he's
soaring...

But he's not.

So, you'll try fetch instead.

When he gets to where
the stick landed,

he'll try to remember
why he's there…

But he can't.

Then you'll ask him what tricks he can do, and he'll tell you he can play dead...

Not only that,
he can roll over...

And over...

And over...

And he'll keep
rolling, until...

He'll tell you he's sure
the dog next door is an
undercover K-9,

and that the two of you should slowly walk into the house...real slow...like nothing's wrong.

Once you're in the house,
he'll tell you that was close...

too close...

and that you'd better
do something to get
rid of the smell.

So, he'll rub...

And rub...

And rub...

Until...

he sees his tail!

He'll chase
his tail...

until his tail
chases him.

When it's over,

he'll tell you that his
mouth is drier than it's
ever been before,

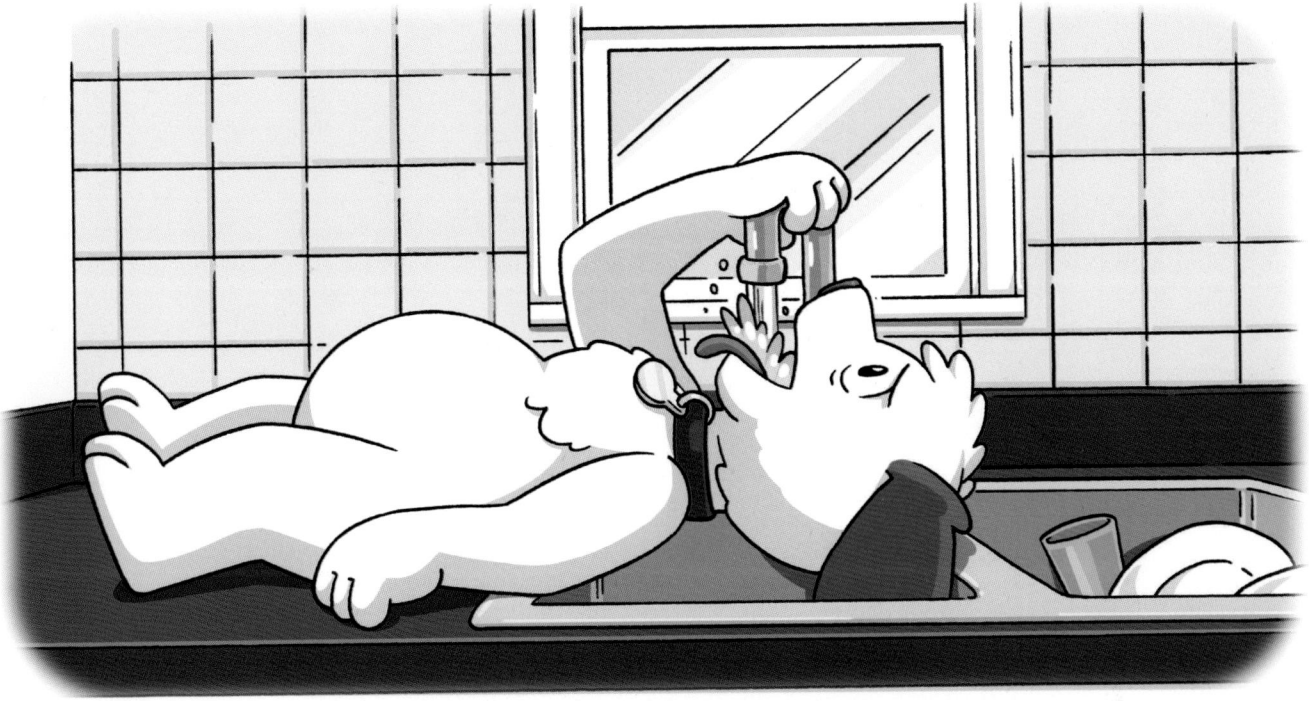

and that he's never been
so thirsty in his life.

The skull and crossbones
in the fish tank will remind him of
the treats he gets at home.

But a dog
doesn't get the
munchies...

He gets the chewies!

He'll be amazed at how much the shoelaces look like ramen noodles, and he'll ask you to take him to the store to buy some.

When he tells you that flying down the road with the wind in his face is the best feeling ever,

you'll tell him the car's still in the driveway.
YOTA
28IF

At the store, he'll ask you
to buy him catnip...

because everyone knows
weed is a gateway drug.

GIFT CARDS
PHARMACY
NIP-NAP
CATTYWHACK

When he asks you
to stop and get tacos
on the way home,

you'll remind him that
you already did.
Talbott's
Tacos

When you get to
a stop sign, he'll tell
you to hold on...

you've got to wait for
it to turn green.

28IF

As soon as
you get home,

he'll want to try
the catnip.

Then he'll play...

And play...

And play...

Until...

he can't play
anymore.
Z
Z
Z
Z
NAP-NAP

The next day when you see him, you'll ask him "Who's a good boy?"

He'll tell you
he is...

But he's not.

Copyright © 2021 by Sam Miserendino

All rights reserved. No part of this book may be reproduced in any manner without the express written consent of the publisher, except in the case of brief excerpts in critical reviews or articles. All inquiries should be addressed to Skyhorse Publishing, 307 West 36th Street, 11th Floor, New York, NY 10018.

Skyhorse Publishing books may be purchased in bulk at special discounts for sales promotion, corporate gifts, fund-raising, or educational purposes. Special editions can also be created to specifications. For details, contact the Special Sales Department, Skyhorse Publishing, 307 West 36th Street, 11th Floor, New York, NY 10018 or info@skyhorsepublishing.com.

Skyhorse® and Skyhorse Publishing® are registered trademarks of Skyhorse Publishing, Inc.®, a Delaware corporation.

Visit our website at www.skyhorsepublishing.com.

10 9 8 7 6 5 4 3 2

Library of Congress Cataloging-in-Publication Data is available on file

Cover and interior artwork by Mike Odum

Print ISBN: 978-1-5107-6101-8

E-book ISBN: 978-1-5107-6595-5

Printed in China

Also Available

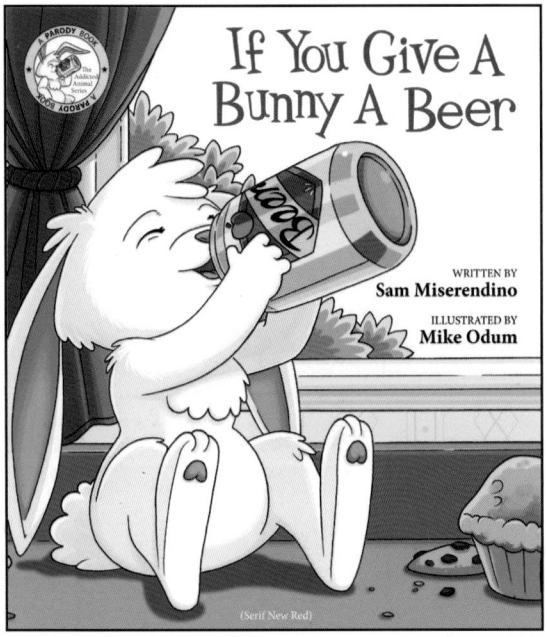

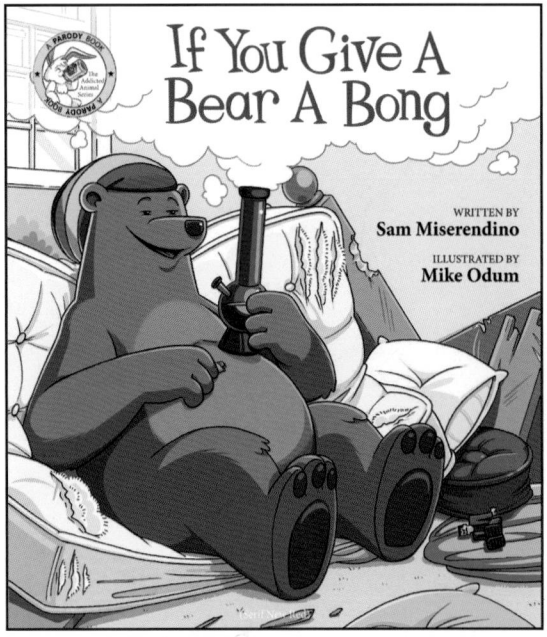

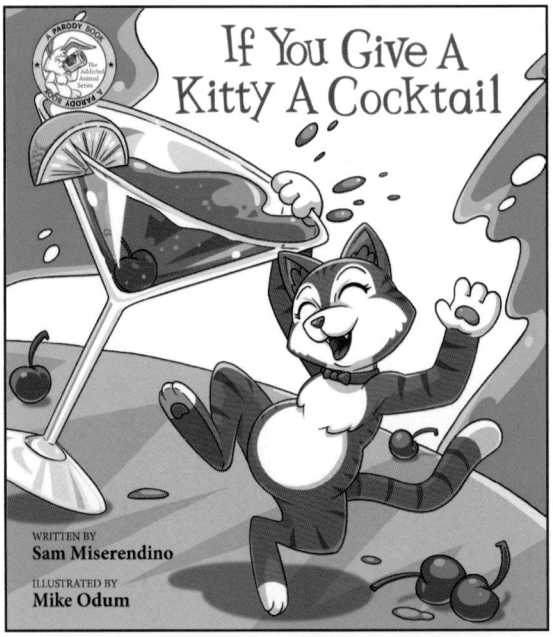